Little Children's Bible Books

RUTH

BROADMAN
&HOLMAN
PUBLISHERS

Retold by Anne de Graaf

Illustrated by José Pérez Montero

RUTH

Published in 2000 by Broadman & Holman Publishers,
Nashville, Tennessee

Text copyright © 2000 Anne de Graaf
Illustration copyright © 2000 José Pérez Montero
Design by Ben Alex
Conceived, designed and produced by Scandinavia Publishing House
Printed in Hong Kong
ISBN 0-8054-2190-4

*Dedicated to Pedro Pérez Rollán
and Madeleine Glennon*

There once was a young woman named Ruth. She married a man from another country and she loved him very much. His mother's name was Naomi.

In which country
were you born?
Is that the same
country you live
in now?

7

Then Ruth's husband died. Naomi told Ruth, "Go back home to your parents." Naomi wanted to go back to the country she had been born in, back to her people, God's people in Israel.

9

Naomi loved God very much.
She had taught her son to love
God. Ruth also loved God
very much.

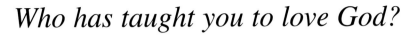
Who has taught you to love God?

11

Ruth begged Naomi, "Please let me go with you, I will go where you go. Your people will be my people and your God, my God. He will take care of us."

13

In what city were you born? Is that the same city you live in now?

Naomi and Ruth walked a long, long way. They walked all the way to Bethlehem, the city where Naomi was born.

When they arrived in Bethlehem, Ruth and Naomi had no food. Ruth wanted to take care of Naomi, so she picked up leftover grain from a field and shared it with Naomi.

Can you find a piece of food that is made from grain? Now share it with the person reading to you.

17

The field Ruth found food in belonged to a man named Boaz. Boaz wanted to help Ruth because she wanted to help Naomi.

So, while Boaz slept under the stars, Ruth curled up at his feet and fell asleep.

One night, Naomi told Ruth she should go to where Boaz was sleeping.

Boaz let Ruth take home as much grain as she wanted. Naomi said, "Does Boaz own the field? He is a relative of mine!"

Naomi told Ruth, "Because Boaz is from my family and cares about us, maybe he will marry you."

27

Boaz was happy to be loved by Ruth. Ruth was happy to be loved by Boaz. They met each other as a part of God's plan for their lives.

Ruth and Boaz were married
and there was a big party.
Naomi was very, very happy!

Have you ever been to a wedding? When was the last time you were very, very happy?

After a while Ruth and Boaz had a little baby boy. They called him "Obed." Now Naomi was like a grandmother to Obed, and this made her very, very happy.

Does someone who loves you have a special name for you?

33

Ruth was a stranger when she came to Bethlehem. But God blessed her because she did what he wanted her to do.

Ruth had left her own people and country out of loyalty and kindness to Naomi. She started with nothing, and now had a husband and son and new home in Bethlehem!

Many, many years later, King David was born in Bethlehem. Many, many years after that, Jesus was born in Bethlehem. And they were both part of the same family, with Obed as a great-great-great grandfather, and Ruth as his mother.

37

A NOTE TO THE big PEOPLE:
The *Little Children's Bible Books* may be your child's first introduction to the Bible, God's Word. This book about Ruth makes that book spring to life. This is a DO book. Point things out and ask your child to find, seek, say, and discover.

Before you read these stories, pray that your child's little heart would be touched by the love of God. These stories are about planting seeds, having vision, learning right from wrong, and choosing to believe. Pray together after you read this. There's no better way for big people to learn from little people.

A little something fun is said in italics by the narrating animal to make the story come alive. In this DO book, wave, wink, hop, roar, or do any of the other things the stories suggest so this can become a fun time of growing closer.